Animal Survival

HOW ANIMALS MOVE

Michel Barré

Gareth Stevens Publishing
MILWAUKEE

For a free color catalog describing Gareth Stevens' list of high-quality books and multimedia programs, call 1-800-542-2595 (USA) or 1-800-461-9120 (Canada). Gareth Stevens Publishing's Fax: (414) 225-0377. See our catalog, too, on the World Wide Web: http://gsinc.com

The editor would like to extend special thanks to Jan W. Rafert, Curator of Primates and Small Mammals, Milwaukee County Zoo, Milwaukee, Wisconsin, for his kind and professional help with the information in this book.

Library of Congress Cataloging-in-Publication Data

Barré, Michel, 1928-
  [Comment se déplacent les animaux? English]
  How animals move / by Michel Barré.
    p. cm. — (Animal survival)
  Includes bibliographical references (p. 47) and index.
  Summary: Describes the various methods of getting around used by different animals and why and how they move as they do.
    ISBN 0-8368-2081-9 (lib. bdg.)
    1. Animal locomotion—Juvenile literature. [1. Animal locomotion.]
  I. Title. II. Series: Barré, Michel, 1928- Animal survival.
  QP301.B34613 1998
  573.7—dc21   97-40155

This North American edition first published in 1998 by
Gareth Stevens Publishing
1555 North RiverCenter Drive, Suite 201
Milwaukee, Wisconsin 53212 USA

This U.S. edition © 1998 by Gareth Stevens, Inc. Original © 1993 by Éditions MANGO-Éditions PEMF, under the French title *Comment se déplacent les animaux?*. Additional end matter © 1998 by Gareth Stevens, Inc.

Translated from the French by Janet Neis.
U.S. editor: Rita Reitci
Editorial assistant: Diane Laska

Series consultant: Michel Tranier, zoologist at the French National Museum of Natural History.

The editors wish to thank the Jacana Agency, and the artists who kindly granted us permission to use the photographs displayed in the following pages:

Cover, Danneger, F. Gohier; 5, J. Robert, Massart; 7, H. Debelius, P. Jaunet; 8, S. de Wilde, Ray Tercafs; 9, Rouxaine; 11, Laboute, Labat-Lanceau, H. Chaumeton, J. M. Labat; 13, J. Lemire, S. de Wilde; 14, Varin-Visage, Arthus-Bertrand, Antony; 15, Y. Lanceau, Frédéric; 17, Varin-Visage, D. Huot; 19, Labat, B. Tournier, R. Dulhoste; 20, A. Carrara, C. Nardin, R. Volot; 23, Varin-Visage; 24, D. Guravich, Frédéric, Veiller; 29, J. Cancalosi, S. Cordier; J. P. Thomas, Varin-Visage, Labat, S. Cordier; 31, A. Deoz, Varin-Visage; 33, Varin-Visage, Bergkessel; 35, C. M. Moiton, J. P. Varin; 37, R. König, J. M. Labat, M. Danegger; 39, J. P. Varin, C. Morel, T. Walker, F. Gohier; 40, Danegger; 41, S. Cordier; 43, C. Nardin, Le Toquin, F. Gohier; 44, Varin-Visage; 45, J. P. Ferrero

Printed in the United States of America

1 2 3 4 5 6 7 8 9 02 01 00 99 98

CONTENTS

WHY DO ANIMALS MOVE AROUND?

To search for food

A few animals can find food without moving. The mussel, for example, filters food from seawater.

Other animals must hunt for their food every day — gathering nectar from flowers, grazing on plants, or hunting and eating other animals.

To flee from predators

Most animals, both the strong and the weak, can become the prey of a predator, which is another animal that hunts prey for food. The hunted animal must flee in order to escape death.

To find a better life

Sometimes local food sources can decrease, or even disappear, for certain animal species. Then the animals must search for a new place to live, where there is enough food and water. This is why some animal species gradually have moved to a great many different places on our planet.

Before each winter, the animals that migrate move to warmer regions to avoid cold weather and to find food. In the spring, these migrators return to their original homes.

To mate

In most animal species, a female can have young only after mating with a male. Often, males and females live apart and come together only in order to reproduce. The males need to search for the females. Some species must travel huge distances to reproduce. Eels and salmon, for example, swim for thousands of miles so they can spawn.

Above: **Gnus flee from a hungry lion on the hunt.**

Opposite: **A reindeer herd moves in search of food.**

4

CONQUERING WATER, EARTH, AND SKY

Above: **A grouper swims over a poisonous stingray lying on the bottom of the sea.**

Scientists have been able to trace the history of today's living beings from as far back as hundreds of millions of years ago. They do this by studying fossils. Fossils are the remains of plants and animals that lived on our planet long ago.

The animal species that we see around us today did not always exist. They originated from older, different species that gradually changed over long periods of time. We call this the evolution of the living world.

Animals and the sea

Over 700 million years ago, the oceans held all our planet's life. The first tiny creatures, of one or a few cells, slowly developed into simple worms and jellyfish. Some later lived in fresh water. These all breathed under water. Crustaceans, mollusks, and even insect ancestors descended from these early animals.

Conquering life on land

Some early animals developed skeletons 600 million years ago and became fish. About 240 million years later, many of these fish evolved into amphibians, the ancestors of frogs and newts. Amphibians, living partly in water and partly on land, could breathe air.

The ancestors of plants and insects began living entirely on land about 400 million years ago.

One million years later, some amphibians evolved into reptiles dwelling on land. Many reptiles developed into dinosaurs and mammals 200 million years ago. Later, some developed into birds.

After the dinosaurs died out 65 million years ago, mammals developed into many different forms. Some gradually returned to the sea to become whales, seals, and other marine mammals. These mammals must go to the surface to breathe air.

Into the air

Insects were the first to fly, 300 million years ago; followed by flying reptiles, such as the now-extinct pterodactyl. Birds evolved about 180 million years ago. They, too, learned to fly, from tiny, hovering hummingbirds to Arctic terns making 22,400-mile (36,000-km) migrations each year. Some birds, such as ostrichs and penguins, cannot fly, but they can run and swim quickly.

Below: **South African springboks graze amid a flock of birds.**

Ways to Move in Water

Invertebrates, animals with no internal skeleton, use various ways to move in water.

Moving by jet

Many invertebrate sea animals, such as jellyfish, cuttlefish, octopus, and squid, use propulsion to move around. This is similar to blowing up a balloon without tying it, then letting it go.

The animal takes water into its body cavity. Then, by contracting its body, it expels the water and shoots backward.

The scallop propels itself by rapidly opening and closing both halves of its shell. The crayfish moves backward using rapid strokes of its tail.

Walking on the bottom

Heavy crustaceans, such as the lobster, usually walk on the sea bottom.

Because of the way its legs are arranged, the crab can walk only sideways.

Sea urchins use some of their spines for walking on the sea bottom.

Starfish use the tube feet on their arms to walk.

Oar strokes

The backswimmer, an insect, uses its two long back legs as oars. At the surface, this bug lies on its back and rows rapidly with its back legs.

Some crabs have back legs that are shaped like oars, which help them swim quickly.

Skating on the surface

Some types of insects, such as the water strider and the water measurer, seem to slide across the water like skaters. Tufts of hair on the ends of their legs gather "air cushions" that work to keep them from sinking into the water.

Above: The octopus takes water into its mantle cavity then expels it, shooting the octopus backward.

Right: The water strider on the surface of the water.

Left: The starfish moves its arms, which are covered underneath with little tube feet.

Opposite: The backswimmer bug swims on its back, using its long back legs as oars.

9

SWIMMING FISH AND FROGS

When swimming, fish do not actually use their fins. They swim by wiggling the flexible back half of their bodies. They use the tail to increase the swaying of the fin.

The other fins, however, are also needed. Without them, a fish could not move in a straight line, turn, or stop. If a fish could not balance its body, it would find itself belly up, as if dead.

Eels and long fish wiggle the whole body from side to side. Flat fish, such as the sole, wiggle up and down. The ray moves in a sort of aquatic flight by slowly flapping its large, triangular fins.

Top: **The ray swims by moving its huge side fins up and down.**

Left: **Some fish move together in groups called schools.**

The gurnard uses its pectoral fins, those on its chest, to "walk" on the sea floor.

Although many types of fish are different in outer appearance from one another, most fish species generally have streamlined bodies so they can move through the water swiftly and easily.

Before becoming frogs, tadpoles swim and breathe with gills under water like fish. Then legs and lungs develop, and the tadpole becomes an adult frog. It lives out of the water but returns to it frequently. The frog is an amphibian, like the salamander and the newt.

The frog swims by extending and contracting its webbed hind legs in a kicking motion, the same movement people use to swim the breast stroke.

Above: **The frog jumps and swims by kicking its back legs.**

Left: **The gurnard can "walk" on its pectoral fins.**

11

SEA MAMMALS: GREAT SWIMMERS

Left: **The sea lion swims with its four flippers.**

Opposite: **The dolphin can leap high out of the water.**

Sea animals, such as the whale and the dolphin, look very much like fish. But they are mammals that nurse their young and must come to the surface of the water to breathe. Scientists call these marine animals cetaceans.

These sea mammals descended from distant mammals that once lived on land but adapted to water life in order to find food. The flippers at the ends of their short arms are "hands" with webbed fingers that look similar to the fins fish have.

Whales and dolphins do not have back legs, but at the end of their tails they have a strong horizontal fin, which helps them dive into the water or come back to the surface. If these animals end up on a beach, they need help to get back to deep water or they will die.

Pinnipeds, such as the walrus, the seal, and the sea lion, are sea mammals with four legs in the shape of flippers.

The walrus moves quickly enough to fight off polar bears.

The seal's back legs, pressed against its tail, are useful only for swimming. On land, it crawls with difficulty, jumping with the help of its front legs.

The sea lion can use its four flippers equally well for swimming and for walking on the ground.

OTHER SWIMMING MAMMALS

Some mammals, such as otters, live near the edge of a small body of water. These animals eat fish and other small mammals.

Otters have webbed feet, which means there is skin between their toes. This webbing helps these animals swim well.

The hippopotamus lives along rivers in Africa. It spends most of its time in the water to avoid the heat. It can walk along the river bottom. The hippopotamus can move its four limbs quickly to swim surprisingly fast.

Swimming ability

Sea mammals swim under water, holding their breath a long time. The sperm whale can hold its breath for over an hour.

Many land mammals, such as the rat, swim out of necessity. Some, such as the dog, swim by choice. Others, such as deer, swim when trying to escape from predators.

Some animals, such as rabbits and cats, do not like to swim.

The chimpanzee can't swim at all and will drown easily if it falls into water.

Many reptiles, such as turtles and crocodiles, are good swimmers. Many snakes swim by wiggling their entire body.

Swimming and seeing

The animals that swim most efficiently near the water's surface, such as crocodiles, hippopotamuses, and frogs, have their eyes and nostrils located on top of their heads. Their bodies are barely visible above the water as they swim. This allows the animals to breathe and to see in front of them without being observed.

Above: **The otter's long body helps it swim well under water.**

Opposite: **The hippopotamus spends most of its time in the water or the mud.**

Above: **Hippopotamus**

Above: **Crocodile**

Above: **Frog**

SWIMMING AND DIVING BIRDS

Birds in the water

The many birds residing near the sea, marshes, or rivers eat plants or animals living in the water.

Some are waders, such as the heron and the stork. These birds have long legs and can walk easily in shallow water.

The dipper is a small bird living in fast-flowing rivers. It walks upstream, its powerful claws holding on to the riverbed as it forages for small insects on the bottom.

The web-footed birds, such as the duck, the swan, and the gull, swim on the surface by paddling with their webbed feet.

Left: **A cormorant under water swims to the surface.**

Unlike the rigid plastic flippers used by human divers, a bird's webbed feet can open and close. During a stroke toward the back, the web unfolds like a fan. Then, to return to the front, it folds up to reduce drag through the water. Some aquatic birds, such as the coot, have thicker lobes of skin between their toes instead of webbing. These lobes of skin act like webbing when the birds swim.

Ducks and swans use their beaks to burrow in the mud by diving into the water and lifting the back ends of their bodies into the air. They can keep their balance in this position with their feet.

To locate food, other birds, such as the petrel, the cormorant, and the water hen, are able to dive completely under the water. The penguin can even use its wings to swim under water.

Above: **This duck tips straight up and down to root in the mud with its beak.**

Below: **A duck's webbed feet act like paddles.**

MOVING WITHOUT WALKING

Pulling up

The earthworm's body is enclosed in rings of muscle, which lengthen and contract separately. Its body also has bristles that point toward the back and can hook firmly into the ground. To move forward, it lengthens its front rings. The earthworm then contracts to drag the rest of its slinky body forward.

Below: **Bands of contraction across this snail's foot show how it moves.**

One-foot movers

If a snail were placed on a plate of glass so it could be observed from below, it would be easy to see the wavy movement of the snail's single foot. This is how it moves.

The clam, a relative of the snail, also has a single foot. It sticks its foot out of its shell, anchors it in the sand, then pulls its entire body forward. This is a slow, clumsy way of getting around, so clams do not move very often.

False feet

Any caterpillar seems to have a lot of feet, but except for the few at the front of its body, these feet are only lumps of flesh, called prolegs.

The prolegs dig into the ground as the caterpillar lengthens or contracts the different parts of its body, moving much the same way as the earthworm does.

Inching along

Having fewer prolegs than some other types of caterpillars, the inchworm caterpillar uses a different method of moving. It lifts and throws the front part of its body forward, hooking the ground with its feet. Then it pulls up the rest of its body into a hump, and starts again.

This resembles the way people measure distances by using their hands, so this caterpillar is called the inchworm.

Above: **Like most caterpillars, this future swallowtail uses its prolegs to move.**

Right: **The inchworm moves by inching along.**

WALKING WITH SIX FEET OR MORE

Insects have six legs. In general, in order to keep its balance while walking, an insect does not lift the three feet on one side or the two feet of a single pair at the same time.

A fly at rest might smooth its wings with its two hind legs. The other four legs keep it balanced.

Spiders have eight legs and move very quickly.

The millipede has two pairs of legs for each of its many sections. Its name, which means "thousand feet," is an exaggeration. It moves its legs one after another, making a wave that travels down the length of its body.

Above: **This beetle, like all insects, walks on six legs.**

Above, left: **The centipede, like the millipede, has many, many feet.**

Left: **This eight-legged harvestman, or daddy longlegs, is related to true spiders.**

21

SNAKES AND OTHER REPTILES

Snakes are reptiles that have no legs or feet. Most snakes travel by wiggling their bodies. The snake moves its head to the right, then to the left, and the rest of its body follows along behind. Its scales, pointing toward the back, allow the snake to move forward only. A snake can lift the front of its body by supporting itself with the rest of its body and its tail. The cobra rises up in this way when it attacks.

Tortoises, crocodiles, and lizards are reptiles that have short legs. Each walks by lifting one foot at a time. The other three legs support it and keep its body off the ground. Moving this way does not slow down the crocodile.

The lizard can move even faster than the heavy crocodile. But the land tortoise moves slowly and has difficulty moving its feet one at a time.

Opposite: **A snake leaves a groove behind it as it crawls.**

Below: **When the crocodile runs, it holds its belly off the ground.**

22

THE DIFFERENT GAITS OF MAMMALS

Various mammal species walk on different parts of their feet.

Walking on soles

Humans walk on the whole foot, from the heel to the toes. Monkeys, badgers, and bears also walk this way.

Scientists describe all animals that walk this way as plantigrades.

Walking on toes

Many carnivorous, or meat-eating, animals move only on the tips of their toes. The underside of the foot has thick pads with claws at the ends.

Scientists describe the animals that walk in this manner as digitigrades. *Digitus* is the Latin word for "digit," another word for finger or toe.

Animals in the cat family are the only digitigrades that can retract, or draw in, their claws when they walk. This keeps their claws from wearing down as they move around.

Walking on nails

Hoofed animals walk on the ends of their toes, which are protected by a thick toenail called a hoof.

Above: **A polar bear's paw (plantigrade)**

Above: **The underside of a cat's paw (digitigrade)**

Above: **A horse's hoof**

Some animals, such as elephants, walk on the five toes of each foot. Others, such as the hippopotamus, have four toes on each foot. The rhinoceros has three toes on each foot. Ruminants, such as cows, deer, and sheep, have two hooves on each foot. Horses and zebras have one hoof on each foot.

Hoof and claw

Animals with hooves are herbivores — they eat plants. They also can run fast for a long time.

This speed is needed to escape predators that hunt them down. These pursuing predators are usually carnivorous digitigrades, meat-eating toe-walkers. Swift and healthy hoofed herbivores can outrun their vicious predators, but the carnivores usually are able to catch the slowest prey — the young, old, or ill.

Above: **This impala, a hoofed herbivore, flees a predator in the African savanna.**

QUADRUPEDS WALKING AND RUNNING

In a slow walk, four-legged animals — called quadrupeds — generally move one front foot, then the diagonally opposite back foot. For example: right front, left back, then left front, right back.

When going faster, the diagonally opposite feet lift nearly together in this pattern: right front and left back, left front and right back, and so on. However, some animals lift both right feet at the same time, then both left feet. This gait, called the amble, is used by the bear, the camel, and the giraffe. Horses also can be taught to walk in this way.

A walking animal must keep at least one foot on the ground at all times for support. When running, there are times when the animal is briefly completely off the ground, with no support.

Horses can run in two different ways: the trot, where the horse lifts its diagonally opposing feet in two stages; and the gallop, where the feet come off the ground in variable order in a three- or four-beat pattern.

Below: **The horse lifts diagonally opposite feet when trotting.**

Analyzing motion

Before the invention of film, artists did not agree on the way a galloping horse lifted its feet.

In the 1870s, Edward Muybridge, an English photographer, had the idea of setting up a series of cameras activated by strings that a horse broke while running. With these amazing photographs, he was able to analyze the movements of various animals and people.

The French physiologist Étienne Marey invented a photographic gun that took successive photos of a bird in flight.

Marey also was interested in many other animals and in people. His work in the 1880s led to the development of the movie camera, which allowed filming at different speeds to better observe and understand movement.

Above, right, boxes 1, 2, 3:
Analysis of different gaits of horses, based on Muybridge's work: 1) walking, 2) trotting, 3) galloping.

Right: **The photographer Muybridge analyzed the movements of animals. Here, a camel ambles.**

JUMPING AND LEAPING

Above: **The kangaroo, propelled by its hind legs, can jump very fast for long distances.**

Some animals move only by continual jumps. The rabbit and the hare stretch out their back legs when they jump and land on their front feet, which are smaller than the back feet.

The kangaroo can move very quickly by jumping with its back legs. It uses its tail to keep its balance while jumping and, at times, to break its landing.

Other animals, such as the flea, the grasshopper, and the frog, frequently move in jumps. All these jumping animals have quick muscle contraction and feet that fold under their legs.

In order to run faster when being pursued by predators, some animals with other gaits, such as the gazelle, can move in long, graceful leaps.

Most carnivores can make a standing jump in order to catch prey or to leap over an obstacle.

Hopping or walking

Birds have only two feet. Some, such as sparrows, can hop only with both feet together. Many other birds walk, often quickly, by moving one foot in front of the other. The chicken and the penguin move in this way. The crow walks when it is not in a hurry but it jumps when it needs to move more quickly.

A champion runner

Although it is too heavy to fly, the ostrich can run as fast as 40 miles (64 km) per hour. Each of its two feet has only two toes. Other birds usually have four toes per foot: three in front, one in back.

Above: **The ostrich cannot fly, but it runs very quickly.**

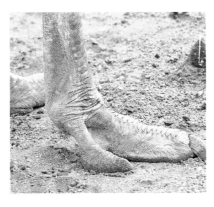

Left: **The ostrich's powerful foot has just two toes.**

CLIMBING AND BURROWING

Many animals can climb. Those with long fingers or toes climb best.

Some animals, such as the tarsier, use their four limbs to hug the branch as they climb.

Monkeys can balance themselves as they travel from branch to branch using hands with thumbs. Spider monkeys do not have thumbs, so they use their tails to grip instead. Anteaters and pangolins climb trees using their four limbs and their tails.

Ways to climb

Animals with short digits need claws to help them climb. Their sharp claws make cats, bears, and sloths expert climbers.

Many climbers, such as squirrels, also jump from branch to branch.

Left: **The tree-dwelling sloth uses its long, curved claws for climbing.**

A fly can remain on a window because of sticky pads at the ends of its feet. The gecko, a small lizard, can climb on walls and even on ceilings. It can do this because its feet have pads with small hair-like structures that grip tiny irregularities on any surface. The geckos are welcome in many Asian homes, where they keep the area free of insects.

Animals do not need feet to be good climbers. Many large snakes, such as boas and pythons, climb trees by winding around the trunk and branches as they crawl upward.

Ways to dig

Some animals can move easily in soil. For example, the earthworm swallows earth as it moves along and expels it as waste after digesting the nourishment it contains. Insect larvae also do this. Some even tunnel through wood, leaving a trail of sawdust.

Many animals dig their burrows in the ground with their front paws, throwing the dirt back with their hind paws. The mole is one of the best diggers, mainly because its strong front paws are built like shovels.

A mole rat digs with its front teeth but does not swallow the dirt.

The vole and the jerboa dig by using their claws. Some desert animals move along by digging their way through the sand.

Below: **The mole digs its burrow with its shovel-shaped forepaws.**

WAYS TO MOVE IN THE AIR

Flights out of water

Many types of fish and some sea mammals, such as dolphins, can leap out of the water, almost as if they were flying.

Flying fish can make "flights" of over 165 feet (50 m) above the water's surface. They can "fly" even farther than this by bouncing on the waves.

Using its tail fin, a flying fish can leap out of the water at great speed and then glide by spreading out its large, wing-like pectoral fins.

Parachute jumping

The flying squirrel and flying lizard cannot really fly. But they both have skin that connects their forefeet and hindfeet. They can stretch out this skin to use as a parachute in order to glide from tree to tree after jumping.

Below: **Flying fish gliding over the waves look like birds.**

Balloon flight

A large balloon can carry extra weight into the air. This also applies to some members of the animal kingdom. For example, young spiders are smaller and lighter than adult spiders. To travel long distances, they make their own "balloons."

A young spider climbs to the top of a plant and secretes a strand of silk from its glands. When the strand is caught by a breeze, the spider rides with it into the air. When the breeze calms, the spider is in a new place. This method of moving is called "ballooning."

Above: **By stretching out the skin that connects its front and hind feet, this squirrel can glide through the air.**

THE FLIGHT OF INSECTS AND BATS

A few insects, such as fleas and lice, never fly. Most insect species have four wings.

The beetle's front wings, called elytra, are stiff, horny plates that cover and protect the back wings. These elytra move aside when the beetle flies.

The mosquito and the fly have only two wings. Two halteres, a pair of tiny stalked knobs, replace the back wings. These help balance the fly and the mosquito in flight.

Insect flight

Flight among insects varies, depending on wing size and how fast the animals can flap. The butterfly flaps its wings nine times per second, the bee flaps its wings 200 times per second, and the midge flaps its wings 1,000 times per second. The dragonfly, with its large, light wings, flies faster than most birds.

Below: **The dragonfly's large, light wings make it a fast-flying insect.**

The hawkmoth and the horsefly are also fast insects. Locusts and some species of butterflies have enough endurance to fly hundreds of miles (km) in long migrations.

A flying mammal

A bat's fingers (except for its thumbs) are very long. They are connected by membranes to form wings. Bats generally fly at about 12 miles (20 km) per hour, but sometimes they can reach 31 miles (50 km) per hour.

Most bats are active at twilight or at night when they hunt for insects. To move around, find prey, and safely avoid obstacles, many bats use a system called echolocation.

A flying bat emits a little piercing cry that bounces off objects and returns as an echo to its large ears. This tells the bat instantly the distance and location of prey or objects to avoid. Large bats living in the tropics are active in daytime and do not use echolocation. Instead, their highly developed eyesight leads them to fruit, nectar, or pollen — the foods they eat.

Some bats migrate, while others hibernate in caves and other dark places.

Above: **The bat flies on wings made by a membrane connecting the long fingers of each hand.**

BIRDS: BEST ADAPTED TO FLIGHT

Some birds, such as the ostrich and the kiwi, do not fly at all. Other birds, such as the chicken, fly poorly. Other birds are excellent flyers.

An aerodynamic shape

The streamlined bodies of good flyers allow them to speed through the air. Water birds, the most streamlined of all, often fly in strong wind.

An ultralight skeleton

A bird's body is solid, but light. The bones in its limbs are hollow and, therefore, less heavy.

Variable wings

Birds fly not only by flapping their wings, but also by twisting them. This produces the greatest power with the least air resistance. An airplane's wings maintain flight only in the air. But a bird's wings also provide the power it needs for flying.

Feathers filter the air

Unlike the bat's solid membranes, a bird's wings are made up of many individual feathers.

The feathers bend with each movement and can filter air. This reduces the turbulence that the bird creates when it moves through the air.

The bird's most powerful muscles are located in its chest. These strong muscles are necessary for flapping the wings.

Stability

Large feathers stabilize the bird's flight, just as a kite's tail steadies the kite.

Feathers also help steer the bird. When the bird lands, it spreads all the feathers of its wings and tail, using them as an air-brake.

Opposite: **The duck brakes with its wings, tail, and feet when coming in for a landing.**

Right: **Fossil imprints of the archaeopteryx, an ancestor of the bird, have been discovered. It lived 150 million years ago. This ancient bird was covered with feathers, but it had a lizard-like jaw.**

Right: **The skeleton of a pigeon with the flight feathers of its wings.**

DIFFERENT WAYS OF FLYING

Flight by flapping

Birds fly by flapping their wings. Every down-stroke of the wings provides a strong thrust that moves the bird ahead. Large birds flap more slowly than smaller birds. The pelican flaps its wings about once per second, the pigeon six or eight times per second, and the titmouse twelve to sixteen times a second.

Gliding and descending

When a bird reaches its flying speed, it can hold

Above: **Like many winged predators, the eagle glides while searching for prey.**

its wings outstretched and glide, descending a little at a time.

All flying birds glide, but the stork and other water birds glide the most.

Birds of prey, such as eagles, hawks, and falcons, and the albatross find warm air currents to lift them up to high altitudes.

The nosedive

Predators, such as the eagle, the falcon, and the sparrowhawk, dive head first to capture their prey. When a gliding bird spots its target, it suddenly plunges down, its wings folded out of the way. When it reaches its victim, the predator extends its feet and air-brakes.

Hovering

The hummingbird is very small — 2 inches (5 centimeters) long. Its tiny wings vibrate seventy times per second, so fast that this bird flies like an insect. Its beating wings make a humming sound.

This bird can fly in any direction, even backward, and can hover in the air like a helicopter.

The hummingbird can drink nectar from flowers without landing on them. The flowers would not be able to support its weight.

Above: **A hummingbird hovers at a flower and drinks its nectar on the wing.**

Below: **A special camera catches three stages of this European robin's flight.**

TAKING OFF AND LANDING

Above: **The swan runs on the water to gain enough speed to take flight.**

Difficult takeoffs

Some large, heavy birds need a running start in order to begin flying. Wetland birds, such as the swan and the duck, "run" on the surface of the water to take flight.

The grounded swift

The swift, a black bird that looks like a large swallow, can sometimes get stuck on the ground, unable to fly. It probably is not injured, but its feet are too short for its wing length, so it cannot take off from the ground.

If it has landed on the ground by mistake, it needs to be tossed gently into the air to gain flight.

Perching

Many birds land on branches and wires. Birds that have one toe opposite the others can do this. The weight of the bird automatically causes its toes to lock around the support on which it lands. Some birds can sleep sitting up on a perch. Predator birds have a grip that allows them to seize prey and carry it away.

Below, right: **A falcon lands on the hand of its tamer, who wears a leather glove to prevent injury.**

Right: **When a bat lands head down, it clings to its perch by squeezing the toes of its hind feet.**

41

ANIMAL MIGRATION

Above: **Placing a band on the leg of a thrush.**

Studying movements

To learn more about the movements of animals, scientists mark them with painless bands that do not interfere with their regular activities. They use nets to capture birds so that bands with the name of the scientific organization and an identification number can be placed on their legs. The birds then are set free again.

Scientists also band bats, place clips on the ears of mammals, put small plaques on fish fins, and insert tubes into whale fat.

Part of an animal's fur or plumage often is painted to follow a specific animal among many similar ones. Sometimes, tiny radio transmitters are attached to animals so that all their movements can be followed accurately.

Since animals don't stay within political borders, scientists of all nations exchange information.

Data transmitted via satellite describes the very

long migrations of some animals. With new data, we can learn more ways to help animals survive.

Annual migrations

Each year, many birds leave their homes in the fall to find winter homes with warmer conditions and a better food supply. In the spring, these birds return to their original homes to reproduce.

Geese living in northern countries fly south to more moderate climates. They fly in a *V*-shaped formation. They take turns flying in the lead and facing the full force of turbulent air.

Whales leave the arctic seas and travel 5,000 miles (8,000 km) south so their young will be born in warm waters. When it is time to reproduce, some schools of fish return to the fresh water or salt water where they hatched.

Migration for life

Young eels are spawned in the Sargasso Sea, an area deep in the Atlantic Ocean. They take from 1-1/2 to 3 years to return to the coast. These elvers then grow into adults in the rivers and swamps of Europe and America.

At the end of their lives, the eels return to the sea where they hatched in order to reproduce. They die after spawning.

Salmon do the opposite. They hatch near the source of a river, then they swim to the sea. They spend most of their lives in salt water. Then they return to the same river from which they came. There they spawn and die.

Above: **Bands come in all sizes to fit different animals.**

Below: **When ready to reproduce, salmon return to the river where they hatched.**

THE DISTRIBUTION OF SPECIES

When there are a great many animals of one species in a region, they spread out to live in nearby areas where they can find food more easily.

Some species, such as African locusts, move in huge groups; others move slowly in small groups.

Many animals cross seas by flying or swimming. They also are often ship passengers, hidden or carried openly. Humans have carried some species to places far from their original homes, often with destructive results. When catfish first traveled to Europe from America and when rabbits first arrived in Australia, the lack of predators caused serious overpopulation problems. These problems are now at least somewhat under control.

Top: **Migrating locusts move in great swarms that damage the vegetation in northern Africa.**

Right: **Millions of introduced rabbits once ravaged Australia's grasslands.**

ANIMAL NAVIGATION

Going by senses

Like humans, animals can see and recognize a familiar environment. They often follow the same trails among the plants of their areas.

Most mammals find their way by using the sense of smell. Dogs are often seen sniffing the ground while they walk. Other animals make use of odors by lifting their heads to smell scents that are carried by the wind.

Experiments done with salmon show that, even when they encounter many small rivers, they can easily recognize the scent of the river where they hatched.

However, pollution can sometimes interfere with this memory.

Sun and stars

Bees can use the Sun's position to find their way back to their hive and also to communicate to other bees the location of any flowers they have found.

Birds, when migrating at night, navigate by the stars. Because of this, they travel more quickly when there are no clouds.

A migrating bird with its internal clock compares its travel time to the time the sun takes to change its position in the sky. This helps it correct the path of its flight.

Carrier pigeons find the direct path back to their dovecotes, even when they have never seen the route they need to follow. Researchers have not yet determined how they are able to do this.

Internal compass

Some experts believe pigeons may be particularly sensitive to Earth's magnetic field, which also attracts the needle on a compass. In other words, they believe the pigeon has some sort of internal compass that guides it to its point of departure.

Below: **Geese fly in a *V*-formation as they migrate.**

GLOSSARY

adapt — to make changes or adjustments in order to survive in a changing habitat or environment.

amble — a way of walking in which an animal moves both right feet at once, then both left feet.

amphibians — cold-blooded vertebrates that are gill-breathers as young and air-breathers as adults. Frogs, toads, and newts are amphibians.

aquatic — living or growing in water.

cavity — a space within a mass; an unfilled space within an animal's body.

contract (*v*)— to pull or squeeze together.

crustaceans — animals with a hard outer shell that live mostly in water. Lobsters and crabs are crustaceans.

digitigrades — animals that walk on the tips of their toes.

endurance — the ability to last a long time, or to withstand hardship or stress.

erratically — having no fixed or regular course.

exaggerate — to enlarge or increase beyond the normal.

expel — to push out or get rid of.

extend — to spread or stretch.

gait — the manner of walking or moving on foot.

glands — organs in the body that make and release substances, such as sweat, tears, poison, and silk.

hatch — to break out of an egg.

hibernate — to enter a state of rest or inactivity in which most bodily functions, such as heartbeat and breathing, slow down. Many animals hibernate during winter.

horizontal — in a position that is level with the horizon.

larva (*pl* **larvae**) — the wingless, wormlike form of a newly hatched insect; the stage coming after the egg but before full development.

mammals — warm-blooded animals that have backbones and hair, bear live young, and produce milk to feed their young.

marine — of or related to the sea.

mate (*v*) — to join together (animals) to produce young.

membrane — a thin, flexible tissue layer or covering in a plant or animal that lines, protects, or stretches over a certain part of its structure.

migrate — to move from one place or climate to another, usually on a seasonal basis.

mollusks — animals with hard, outer shells, usually living in water, such as clams and snails.

plantigrades — animals that walk on the whole foot, from heel to toe.

predators — animals that hunt and eat other animals.

prey — animals that are hunted and eaten by others.

quadrupeds — animals with four legs.

reproduce — to create offspring.

secrete — to form and give off a substance of some kind, usually liquid.

spawn — to release eggs in the water.

species — animals or plants that are closely related and often similar in behavior and appearance. Members of the same species are capable of breeding together.

stabilize — to prevent excessive rolling and produce a smooth movement.

streamlined — shaped so as to reduce resistance to motion when traveling through air or water.

BOOKS TO READ

Animal Journeys. Joyce Pope
(Troll Communications)

Animal Magic series. (Gareth Stevens)

Animal Movement. Jill Bailey and
Tony Seddon (Facts on File)

Animal Movement. Jim Flegg (Newington)

Animal Travelers. Jim Flegg (Newington)

Animals on the Move. Mark Carwardine
(Garrett Educational)

The Living Pond. Nathalie Tordjman
(Young Discovery Library)

Mammal Migration. Liz Oram and
Robin Baker (Raintree Steck-Vaughn)

The New Creepy Crawly Collection series.
(Gareth Stevens)

*One Hundred One Wacky Facts about Bugs
and Spiders.* Brian Hendryx (Scholastic)

Really Radical Reptiles and Amphibians.
Leslee Elliott (Sterling)

Secrets of the Animal World series.
(Gareth Stevens)

Through the Air: Life on the Move.
Seymour Simon (Harcourt Brace)

A Walk on the Great Barrier Reef.
Caroline Arnold (Lerner Group)

Wonderful World of Animals series.
Beatrice MacLeod (Gareth Stevens)

VIDEOS

Animals Move from Here to There.
(Pyramid Media)

Animals Move in Many Ways.
(Phoenix/BFA Films & Video)

Birds of Prey. (Rainbow Educational Media)

How Animals Move.
(Agency for Instructional Technology)

Insects and Spiders Up Close.
(Hatch, Warren Productions)

WEB SITES

www.ducks.org/puddler/frame_special.html

www.bev.net/education/SeaWorld/
manatees.html

www.5tigers.org/coolfac.htm

www.bev.net/education/SeaWorld/
coral_reefs/introcr.html

INDEX